Images from the
BIBLE
The New Testament

Bilder aus der Bibel *Das Neue Testament*
Images de la Bible *Nouveau Testament*
Imágenes de la Biblia *El Nuevo Testamento*

For permission to use images in this book and CD-ROM, please contact the publishers. Unauthorized use will be subject to legal proceedings, and the charging of all costs involved and a penalty.

The Pepin Press BV
P.O. Box 10349
1001 EH Amsterdam
The Netherlands

T +31 20 420 20 21
F +31 20 420 11 52
mail@pepinpress.com
www.pepinpress.com

All images in this book are from The Pepin Press image archive.

Concept and cover design: Pepin van Roojen
Picture and text editing and layout: Kevin Haworth
Design consultants: Maria da Gandra and Maaike van Neck

Translations: Sebastian Viebahn (DE), chasingwords.nl (FR)
and LocTeam (ES)

ISBN 978-90-5768-136-3

2016 15 14 13 12 11 10
10 9 8 7 6 5 4 3 2 1

Manufactured in Singapore

Captions for images on pages 3, 4, 6, 8 & 10:

page 4:
Jesus in heaven with the patriarchs and saints. Moses can be seen with the tablets of the law and commands, and Abraham with a sacrificial knife.
Jesus im Himmel mit den Erzvätern und Heiligen. Moses hält die Gesetzestafeln und Abraham ein Opfermesser.
Jésus au ciel entouré des patriarches et des saints. On aperçoit Moïse avec les tables de la loi et Abraham avec un couteau sacrificiel.
Jesús en el cielo con los patriarcas y los santos. Moisés sostiene las tablas de la ley y Abraham un cuchillo de sacrificio.

pages 3 & 6:
The Holy Trinity: God the father, Jesus holding the cross, and the Holy Spirit in the form of a dove
Die heilige Dreifaltigkeit: Gottvater, Jesus mit dem Kreuz und der Heilige Geist als Taube
La Sainte Trinité : Dieu, le Père, Jésus tenant la croix et le Saint Esprit sous la forme d'une colombe
La Santísima Trinidad: Dios Padre, Jesús sosteniendo la cruz y el Espíritu Santo en forma de paloma

page 8:
Angels rejoicing as the cross of Jesus defeats death
Engel bejubeln den Sieg des Kreuzes Christi über den Tod
Les anges se réjouissent car la croix de Jésus a vaincu la mort
Los ángeles se regocijan con el triunfo de la cruz sobre la muerte

page 10:
A depiction of (from bottom to top) the immaculate conception, the birth of Jesus, His resurrection and His ascension into heaven. The triangle at the top symbolizes the Holy Trinity, and the angel, lion, ox and eagle on either side represent the 4 writers of the gospels.
Darstellungen (von oben nach unten) der Unbefleckten Empfängnis, von Jesu Geburt, der Auferstehung und der Himmelfahrt. Das Dreieck oben symbolisiert die Heilige Dreifaltigkeit. Engel, Löwe, Ochse und Adler auf beiden Seiten stehen für die 4 Verfasser der Evangelien.
Représentation (de bas en haut) de l'Immaculée Conception, la naissance de Jésus, sa résurrection et son ascension. Le triangle, en haut, symbolise la Sainte Trinité. L'ange, le lion, le bœuf et l'aigle situés de chaque côté représentent les auteurs des 4 évangiles.
Representación (de abajo arriba) de la Inmaculada Concepción, el nacimiento de Jesús, su resurrección y su ascensión al cielo. El triángulo superior simboliza la Santísima Trinidad. El ángel, el león, el buey y el águila representan a los 4 evangelistas.

Contents

Free CD inside the back cover

CD and Image Rights

Introduction

Bible stories – and the pictures that illustrate them – are an integral part of the cultural heritage of Europe. When European colonists spread their cultures and religions around the world, the cultural, visual and artistic references associated with these Bible stories travelled with them. References to Bible stories – such as the prodigal son and the good Samaritan – can be found in art, literature and everyday expressions in cultures around the world.

Countless histories and retellings of the Bible exist in nearly every language on Earth today. This collection does not attempt to recount or interpret the stories of the Bible. It is a collection of images and illustrations – by a variety of artists and in a range of styles – that have influenced and continue to influence art and culture around the world.

The images in this book were selected from antique and rare Bibles and Bible-related books in the Pepin Press archive that were published between 1701 and 1909. The illustrations date from the 17th to the 19th century. Many of the artists, engravers and woodcutters who made these images have faded into the anonymity of history. One notable exception is Gustave Doré (1832–1883), an influential artist, engraver, and illustrator in Paris and London in the 19th century. A good number of illustrations from his Bible (1866) can be found in this collection.

The birth of Jesus
Die Geburt Jesu
Naissance de Jésus
El nacimiento de Jesús

Wise men from the East bring gifts for Jesus
Weise aus dem Morgenland bringen Jesus Geschenke
Des mages venus d'Orient apportent des présents à Jésus
Los Reyes Magos traen presentes a Jesús

CD und Bildrechte

Alle Abbildungen in diesem Buch sind auf der beigelegten CD gespeichert und können als Anregung oder Ausgangsmaterial für Designzwecke genutzt werden. Alle Bilddateien auf den CDs von Pepin Press sind so groß dimensioniert, dass sie für die meisten Anwendungszwecke ausreichen. Die Namen der einzelnen Bilddateien auf der CD entsprechen den Seitenzahlen und/oder den Bildzahlen im Buch. Auf Anfrage können Dateien und/oder Vektordateien der meisten Bilder bei The Pepin Press bestellt werden.

Als Käufer dieses Buchs dürfen Sie die Bilder auf der CD kostenfrei nutzen für:
• sämtliche privaten, nicht professionellen und nicht-kommerziellen Anwendungen
• zum Zweck des Webdesign (bis max. 10 Bilder pro Projekt) und/oder
• für kommerzielle Zwecke in kleinem Rahmen (z.B. Broschüren mit einer Druckauflage von max. 5.000 Exemplaren bei einer Nutzung von max. 5 Bildern aus diesem Buch)

Dagegen muss eine Genehmigung eingeholt werden bei der Nutzung der Bilder:
• in anderen Publikationen
• für kommerzielle Zwecke in großem Rahmen
• zur Dekoration von Luxusgütern und/oder
• in Werbekampagnen

In Zweifelsfällen bitten wir Sie, uns zu kontaktieren: Im Normalfall erteilen wir solche Genehmigungen recht großzügig und erheben - wenn überhaupt - nur geringe Gebühren. In jedem Fall freuen wir uns über Arbeitsproben, in denen unser Bildmaterial verwendet wurde.

Darüber hinaus ist jede weitere Verbreitung von Pepin Press-Materialien in jeglicher Form, Art und Weise untersagt.

Für weitere Informationen über Genehmigungen und Gebühren wenden Sie sich bitte an:
mail@pepinpress.com
Fax: +31 20 4201152

Einführung

Die Erzählungen der Bibel und die Bilder aus Bibelillustrationen sind ein Teil des europäischen Kulturerbes. In der Kolonialzeit exportierten die Europäer mit ihren Kulturen und ihrem Glauben auch kulturelle, visuelle und künstlerische Elemente der Bibelerzählungen. Biblische Begriffe wie Judaskuss oder verlorener Sohn durchziehen deshalb heutzutage Kunst, Literatur und Alltagssprache in Kulturen rund um den Globus.

Heute gibt es in fast jeder Sprache der Welt zahllose Bibelerzählungen und -nacherzählungen. Diese Reihe interpretiert aber weder Bibelgeschichten noch erzählt sie sie neu, sondern versammelt Bilder und Illustrationen - von unterschiedlichsten Künstlern und in verschiedensten Stilen -, die bis in die Gegenwart hinein weltweit Kunst und Kultur beeinflusst haben.

Die Bilder in diesem Band entstammen alten, seltenen Bibelausgaben oder thematisch verwandten Büchern aus dem Pepin Press-Archiv, die zwischen 1701 und 1909 erschienen sind. Die Illustrationen dazu entstanden im 17. bis 19. Jahrhundert. Von den Zeichnern, Kupferstechern und Holzschneidern, die sie schufen, sind viele inzwischen in Vergessenheit geraten. Eine bemerkenswerte Ausnahme bildet Gustave Doré (1832-1883), ein einflussreicher Maler, Grafiker und Illustrator, der in Paris und London arbeitete. Viele Illustrationen aus seiner 1866 erschienen Bibel finden sich in dieser Sammlung.

The devil tempts Jesus in the wilderness
Der Teufel versucht Jesus in der Wildnis
Le diable tente Jésus dans le désert
El demonio tienta a Jesús en el desierto

Jesus meets Zacchaeus in Jericho
Jesus begegnet Zachäus bei Jericho
Jésus rencontre Zachée près de Jéricho
Jesús conoce a Zaqueo en Jericó

CD et droits relatifs aux images

Les images de ce livre sont également incluses dans le CD qui l'accompagne et sont exploitables comme source d'inspiration ou de base à un document. Les fichiers contenus sur les CD de The Pepin Press sont de taille suffisamment grande pour convenir à la plupart des usages et le nom des fichiers correspond au numéro des pages et/ou des images du livre. De nombreuses illustrations sont proposées sous forme de fichiers de taille plus importante et/ou vectorisées, que vous pouvez commander auprès de The Pepin Press.

Si vous avez acheté ce livre, vous pouvez utiliser à titre gratuit les images contenues dans le CD pour :
• tous les usages privés, non professionnels et non commerciaux ;
• la réalisation de sites Web utilisant au maximum 10 images par site et/ou ;
• les usages commerciaux de type artisanal (par exemple : brochures tirées à moins de 5 000 exemplaires et reprenant au plus 5 images).

Une autorisation est nécessaire pour l'utilisation des images :
• dans d'autres publications ;
• pour un usage commercial de grande envergure ;
• pour la décoration d'articles de luxe et/ou ;
• dans le cadre de campagnes publicitaires à grande diffusion.

En cas de doute, veuillez nous contacter. Notre politique d'autorisation est très accommodante et nos frais pratiqués, le cas échéant, sont minimes. Dans tous les cas, nous sommes intéressés de recevoir des exemples de mises en œuvre de nos images.

Toute autre distribution de documents de The Pepin Press sous quelque forme et par quelque moyen que ce soit est interdite.

Pour toute demande de renseignements sur les autorisations et les frais, veuillez contacter :
mail@pepinpress.com
Fax : +31 20 4201152

Introduction

Les histoires bibliques – et les images qui les illustrent – font partie intégrante de l'héritage culturel européen. Lorsque les colons européens ont répandu leurs cultures et religions à travers le monde, les références culturelles, visuelles et artistiques associées à ces histoires bibliques ont également été véhiculées. Des références aux histoires bibliques – telles que le fils prodigue et le bon Samaritain – sont présentes dans l'art, la littérature et les expressions de tous les jours dans les cultures du monde entier.

Il existe aujourd'hui d'innombrables histoires et adaptations de la Bible dans pratiquement toutes les langues de la Terre. Ce recueil n'a pas pour ambition de narrer ou interpréter les histoires de la Bible. Il s'agit d'une collection d'images et d'illustrations – réalisées par une grande diversité d'artistes et dans différents styles – qui ont influencé et continuent d'influencer l'art et la culture à travers le monde.

Les images figurant dans ce livre ont été sélectionnées dans des Bibles anciennes et rares ainsi que dans des livres consacrés à la Bible, parmi les archives de Pepin Press, qui ont été publiés entre 1701 et 1909. Les illustrations remontent au 17ème et au 19ème siècle. Un grand nombre des artistes, graveurs et sculpteurs sur bois, auteurs de ces images, ont disparu dans l'anonymat de l'Histoire. Il existe toutefois une exception notable : Gustave Doré (1832–1883). Gustave Doré était un artiste, graveur et illustrateur influent à Paris et à Londres au 19ème siècle. Ce recueil renferme un grand nombre des illustrations tirées de sa Bible (1866).

The widow's offering
Das Scherflein der Witwe
L'offrande de la veuve
El óbolo de la viuda

Jesus heals a man at the pool called Bethesda
Jesus heilt einen Mann am Teich Betesda
Jésus guérit un paralytique à la piscine appelée Bethesda
Jesús sana a un paralítico en la piscina de Betesda

9

John Hookes of Conway in
Carnarvon Shire Knoll of Stockwell
in the County of Surrey Gent
For advancement of this Worke
contributed this Plate.

CD y derechos de las imágenes

Las imágenes que contiene este libro están incluidas en el CD adjunto y pueden utilizarse como inspiración o referencia para el diseño. Los archivos incluidos en los CD de The Pepin Press tienen un tamaño suficiente para la mayoría de las aplicaciones, y los nombres de archivo se corresponden con los números de página o de imagen utilizados en el libro. Para muchas de las imágenes hay disponibles archivos más grandes o archivos vectoriales, que pueden encargarse a The Pepin Press.

Si ha comprado este libro, puede utilizar libremente las imágenes incluidas en el CD para:
• cualquier propósito particular, no profesional y no comercial;
• diseño web, siempre que utilice un máximo de 10 imágenes por proyecto;
• uso comercial de poca envergadura (por ejemplo, folletos con una tirada inferior a los 5.000 ejemplares en los que no se usen más de cinco imágenes nuestras).

Se necesita autorización para la utilización de las imágenes:
• en otras publicaciones;
• para un uso comercial de amplia difusión;
• para la decoración de artículos de lujo;
• en campañas publicitarias importantes.

En caso de duda, le rogamos que se ponga en contacto con nosotros. Nuestra política de autorización es muy razonable y, en los casos en que se aplican tarifas, estas tienden a ser mínimas. En cualquier caso, agradecemos que nos envíen ejemplos de trabajos en los que se hayan utilizado nuestras imágenes.

Queda prohibida toda distribución de material de The Pepin Press que exceda de cualquier modo los límites mencionados.

Para consultas sobre autorizaciones y tarifas, póngase en contacto con:
mail@pepinpress.com
Fax: +31 20 4201152

Introducción

Las historias de la Biblia y las imágenes que las ilustran son parte integrante del patrimonio cultural de Europa. Cuando los colonizadores europeos difundieron sus culturas y religiones por el mundo, también llevaron consigo las referencias culturales, visuales y artísticas asociadas a estas historias bíblicas. Tales referencias, como el buen samaritano y el hijo pródigo, se encuentran en el arte, la literatura y las expresiones corrientes de culturas de todo el mundo.

Aún hoy en día, casi todos los idiomas conservan incontables referencias bíblicas. Esta recopilación no pretende relatar o interpretar todas las historias de la Biblia; más bien es una colección de imágenes e ilustraciones, realizadas por diversos artistas en un abanico de estilos diferentes, que han influido y siguen influyendo en el arte y la cultura de nuestro planeta.

Las imágenes de este libro fueron escogidas de entre las ilustraciones de ejemplares antiguos y peculiares de la Biblia y de otros libros relacionados con ella del archivo de Pepin Press, publicados entre 1701 y 1909. Así, las ilustraciones datan de los siglos XVII al XIX. Muchos de los artistas y grabadores que crearon estas imágenes han caído en el anonimato de la historia. Una notable excepción es Gustave Doré (1832-1883), un influyente artista, grabador e ilustrador que trabajó en París y Londres durante el siglo XIX. Este libro incluye un buen número de ilustraciones de su Biblia (1866).

The dragon pursues the woman of the Apocalypse
Der Drache verfolgt die Frau aus der Apokalypse
Le dragon poursuit la femme de l'Apocalypse
El dragón persigue a la mujer del Apocalipsis

The triumph of Jesus' cross over death
Der Triumph des Kreuzes Christi über den Tod
La croix de Jésus triomphant de la mort
El triunfo de la cruz de Jesús sobre la muerte

↑
Mary, Jesus and adoring angels. The snake represents Satan.
Maria, Jesus und betende Engel. Satan ist als Schlange dargestellt.
Marie, Jésus et les anges en adoration. Satan représenté par un serpent.
María, Jesús y unos ángeles. La serpiente representa a Satán.

→
Jesus with a crown of thorns
Jesus mit einer Dornenkrone
Jésus avec la couronne d'épines
Jesús con una corona de espinas

←

Jesus surrounded by his followers. In the lower left corner, the evangelists can be identified by the symbolic angel, lion, ox and eagle. John the Baptist (holding a banner) and Saint Paul (with sword and quill) are in the lower right corner.

Jesus inmitten seiner Anhänger. Unten links sind die Evangelisten durch Engel, Löwe, Ochse und Adler symbolisiert. Unten rechts Johannes der Täufer (mit einem Banner) und Paulus (mit Schwert und Feder).

Jésus entouré de ses disciples. Dans l'angle inférieur gauche, les évangélistes sont symbolisés par l'ange, le lion, le bœuf et l'aigle. Jean le Baptiste (tenant une bannière) et Saint Paul (avec épée et plume) sont dans l'angle inférieur droit

Jesús rodeado de seguidores. En la esquina inferior izquierda están los evangelistas, reconocibles por el ángel, el león, el buey y el águila. En la esquina inferior derecha están san Juan Bautista (con un estandarte) y san Pablo (con espada y una pluma).

↑

The writers of the 4 gospels: Matthew, Mark, Luke and John
Die Verfasser der 4 Evangelien: Matthäus, Markus, Lukas und Johannes
Les auteurs des 4 évangiles : Matthieu, Marc, Luc et Jean
Los autores de los 4 Evangelios: Mateo, Marcos, Lucas y Juan

 The evangelist Matthew, traditionally shown with an angel
Der Evangelist Matthäus, üblicherweise mit einem Engel dargestellt
L'évangéliste Matthieu, généralement représenté par un ange
San Mateo evangelista, representado tradicionalmente por un ángel

 The evangelist Mark, traditionally shown with a lion
Der Evangelist Markus, üblicherweise mit einem Löwen dargestellt
L'évangéliste Marc, généralement représenté par un Lion
San Marcos evangelista, representado tradicionalmente por un león

↑   ↑

The evangelist Luke, traditionally shown with an ox

Der Evangelist Lukas, üblicherweise mit einem Ochsen dargestellt

L'évangéliste Luc, généralement représenté par un bœuf

San Lucas evangelista, representado tradicionalmente por un buey

The evangelist John, traditionally shown with an eagle

Der Evangelist Johannes, üblicherweise mit einem Adler dargestellt

L'évangéliste Jean, généralement représenté par un aigle

San Juan evangelista, representado tradicionalmente por un águila

↑

The evangelist Matthew, traditionally shown with an angel
Der Evangelist Matthäus, üblicherweise mit einem Engel dargestellt
L'évangéliste Matthieu, généralement représenté par un ange
San Mateo evangelista, representado tradicionalmente por un ángel

The evangelist Mark, traditionally shown with a lion
Der Evangelist Markus, üblicherweise mit einem Löwen dargestellt
L'évangéliste Marc, généralement représenté par un Lion
San Marcos evangelista, representado tradicionalmente por un león

To her Sacred Majesty Katharine Queen Dowager of England &c. This Plate in all humility is most humbly dedicated by y.e Majestys most obedient Serv.e ant Richard Blome

↑
The evangelist Luke, traditionally shown with an ox
Der Evangelist Lukas, üblicherweise mit einem Ochsen dargestellt
L'évangéliste Luc, généralement représenté par un bœuf
San Lucas evangelista, representado tradicionalmente por un buey

20

To his Royall High ... ness George Prince of
Denmark
This Plate is most &c
by the Royall Humbly Dedicated
obedient Servant Highnesses most
Richard Blome

↑
The evangelist John, traditionally shown with an eagle
Der Evangelist Johannes, üblicherweise mit einem Adler dargestellt
L'évangéliste Jean, généralement représenté par un aigle
San Juan evangelista, representado tradicionalmente por un águila

The four evangelists can be identified by the symbols in the image: the angel, lion, ox and eagle
Die vier Evangelisten, zu erkennen anhand ihrer Symbole: Engel, Löwe, Ochse und Adler
Les quatre évangélistes peuvent être identifiés par les symboles de l'ange, du lion, du bœuf et de l'aigle
Los cuatro evangelistas se pueden identificar por sus símbolos: el ángel, el león, el buey y el águila

Paul, sometimes referred to as the apostle to the Gentiles
Paulus, manchmal bezeichnet als Apostel der Nichtjuden
Paul, parfois appelé l'Apôtre des Gentils
San Pablo, a veces llamado el apóstol de los gentiles

The 12 apostles and Paul
Die 12 Apostel mit Paulus
Les 12 Apôtres et Paul
Los 12 apóstoles y san Pablo

Symbolism:
In Christian art, apostles can often be identified by the symbol(s) traditionally associated with them. For example, Paul is usually depicted with a sword and often a book (or scroll), and Peter with a key.

Symbolik:
In der christlichen Kunst sind die Apostel oft an ihren Attributen zu erkennen. Paulus etwa wird meist mit Schwert, oft auch mit Buch (oder Rolle) dargestellt, Petrus mit einem Schlüssel.

Symbolisme :
L'art chrétien représente souvent les apôtres par des symboles qui permettent de les identifier. Par exemple, Paul est souvent représenté avec une épée et un livre (ou parchemin) et Pierre avec une clé.

Simbolismo:
En el arte cristiano, los apóstoles se suelen identificar por los símbolos asociados tradicionalmente a ellos. Por ejemplo, Pablo y la espada y, con frecuencia, un libro (o pergamino), y Pedro y la llave.

Peter, also called Simon or Simon Peter
Petrus, auch Simon oder Simon Petrus genannt
Pierre, également appelé Simon ou Simon Pierre
Simón, apodado Pedro

Andrew, brother of Simon Peter
Andreas, Bruder des Simon Petrus
André, frère de Simon Pierre
Andrés, hermano de Pedro

James, son of Zebedee
Jakobus, Sohn des Zebedäus
Jacques, fils de Zébédée
Santiago el Mayor, hijo de Zebedeo

John, son of Zebedee
Johannes, Sohn des Zebedäus
Jean, fils de Zébédée
Juan, hijo de Zebedeo

Philip
Philippus
Philippe
Felipe

Bartholomew, also called Nathanael
Bartholomäus, auch Natanaël genannt
Barthélémy, également appelé Nathanaël
Bartolomé, llamado también Natanael

Matthew, also called Levi
Matthäus, auch Levi genannt
Matthieu, également appelé Lévi
Mateo, también llamado Leví

Thomas, sometimes called Doubting Thomas
Thomas, mitunter der ungläubige Thomas genannt
Thomas, également appelé Thomas l'Incrédule
Tomás, a veces apodado el Incrédulo

James, son of Alphaeus, also called James the Just
Jakobus, Sohn des Alphäus, auch Jakobus der Gerechte genannt
Jacques, fils d'Alphée, également appelé Jacques le Juste
Santiago el Menor, hijo de Alfeo, apodado el Justo

Simon or Simon the Zealot
Simon, auch Simon der Zelot genannt
Simon ou Simon le Zélote
Simón, apodado el Zelote

Jude, also called Thaddeus
Judas, auch Judas Thaddäus genannt
Jude, également appelé Thaddée
Judas, también llamado Tadeo

Matthias, who replaced Judas Iscariot
Matthias, der den Judas Iskariot ersetzte
Matthias, qui remplace Judas l'Iscariote
Matías, el sucesor de Judas Iscariote

↑
Jesus gives Peter the key to the kingdom of heaven
Jesus übergibt Petrus den Schlüssel zum Reich Gottes
Jésus donne à Pierre les clés du Royaume des Cieux
Jesús da a Pedro la llave del reino de los cielos

The 7 virtues: Faith, Hope and Love
Die 7 Tugenden: Glaube, Hoffnung und Liebe
Les 7 vertus : Foi, Espérance et Charité
Las 7 virtudes: fe, esperanza y caridad

↑
The 7 virtues: Prudence, Justice, Courage and Restraint
Die 7 Tugenden: Klugheit, Gerechtigkeit, Tapferkeit und Mäßigung
Les 7 vertus : Prudence, Justice, Force et Temperance
Las 7 virtudes: prudencia, justicia, templanza y fortaleza

The 7 deadly sins: Pride
Die 7 Todsünden: Hochmut
Les 7 péchés capitaux : Orgueil
Las 7 pecados capitales: soberbia

AVARICE

JUDAS VEND NOTRE-SEIGNEUR

LUXURE

L'ENFANT PRODIGUE

GOURMANDISE

LE DROIT D'AINESSE VENDV POVR VN PLAT DE LENTILLES

↑
The 7 deadly sins: Greed, Lust and Gluttony
Die 7 Todsünden: Habgier, Wollust, Völlerei
Les 7 péchés capitaux : Avarice, Luxure et Gourmandise
Las 7 pecados capitales: avaricia, lujuria y gula

30

ENVIE

JOSEPH VENDV PAR SES FRERES

COLERE

COLERE D'ESAV CONTRE JACOB

PARESSE

LE CHAMP DV PARESSEVX

The 7 deadly sins: Envy, Wrath and Sloth
Die 7 Todsünden: Neid, Zorn, Trägheit
Les 7 péchés capitaux : Envie, Colère et Paresse
Las 7 pecados capitales: envidia, ira y pereza

Map: Canaan and the travels of Jesus and His apostles
Karte: Kanaan und die Reisen Jesu und seiner Apostel
Carte : Canaan et les voyages de Jésus et de ses apôtres
Mapa: Canaán y los viajes de Jesús y sus apóstoles

↑

Gabriel appears to Zechariah and foretells the birth of John the Baptist
Gabriel kündigt Zacharias die Geburt von Johannes dem Täufer an
Gabriel apparaît à Zacharie et lui annonce la naissance de Jean le Baptiste
Gabriel se aparece a Zacarías y anuncia el nacimiento de san Juan el Bautista

→

Gabriel appears to Mary and foretells the birth of Jesus
Gabriel erscheint Maria und kündigt ihr Jesu Geburt an
Gabriel apparaît à Marie et annonce la naissance de Jésus
Gabriel se aparece a María y anuncia el nacimiento de Jesús

⇞ ↑ →
Gabriel appears to Mary and foretells the birth of Jesus
Gabriel erscheint Maria und kündigt ihr Jesu Geburt an
Gabriel apparaît à Marie et annonce la naissance de Jésus
Gabriel se aparece a María y anuncia el nacimiento de Jesús

↑
Gabriel appears to Mary and foretells the birth of Jesus
Gabriel erscheint Maria und kündigt ihr Jesu Geburt an
Gabriel apparaît à Marie et annonce la naissance de Jésus
Gabriel se aparece a María y anuncia el nacimiento de Jesús

An angel visits Joseph in a dream and foretells the birth of Jesus
Josef erscheint ein Engel im Traum und kündigt ihr Jesu Geburt an
Un ange apparaît à Joseph dans un songe et annonce la naissance de Jésus
Un ángel visita a José en sueños y anuncia el nacimiento de Jesús

Mary visits Elizabeth, mother of John the Baptist
Maria besucht Elisabet, die Mutter von Johannes dem Täufer
Marie rend visite à Elisabeth, mère de Jean le Baptiste
María visita a Isabel, madre de san Juan el Bautista

Elizabeth and the infant John the Baptist
Elisabet mit Johannes dem Täufer als Kind
Elisabeth et son enfant Jean le Baptiste
Isabel y san Juan el Bautista de niño

An angel visits Joseph in a dream
Josef erscheint ein Engel im Traum
Un ange apparaît à Joseph dans un songe
Un ángel visita a José en sueños

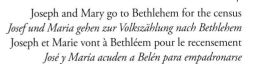

Joseph and Mary go to Bethlehem for the census
Josef und Maria gehen zur Volkszählung nach Bethlehem
Joseph et Marie vont à Bethléem pour le recensement
José y María acuden a Belén para empadronarse

The birth of Jesus
Die Geburt Jesu
Naissance de Jésus
El nacimiento de Jesús

Angels announce Jesus' birth to shepherds in the fields
Engel verkünden den Hirten auf dem Feld Jesu Geburt
Des anges annoncent la naissance de Jésus aux bergers dans les champs
Varios ángeles anuncian el nacimiento de Jesús a los pastores

Shepherds come to worship Jesus
Hirten kommen Jesus anzubeten
Les bergers viennent adorer Jésus
Los pastores van a adorar a Jesús

↟

An angel announces Jesus' birth to shepherds in the fields
Ein Engel verkündet den Hirten auf dem Feld Jesu Geburt
Un ange annonce la naissance de Jésus aux bergers dans les champs
Un ángel anuncia el nacimiento de Jesús a los pastores

← ↑

Shepherds come to to worship Jesus
Hirten kommen Jesus anzubeten
Les bergers viennent adorer Jésus
Los pastores van a adorar a Jesús

Angels announce Jesus' birth to shepherds in the fields
Engel verkünden den Hirten auf dem Feld Jesu Geburt
Des anges annoncent la naissance de Jésus aux bergers dans les champs
Varios ángeles anuncian el nacimiento de Jesús a los pastores

Simeon blesses Jesus in the temple
Simeon segnet Jesus im Tempel
Syméon bénit Jésus dans le temple
Simeón bendice a Jesús en el Templo

↑
Shepherds come to worship Jesus
Hirten kommen Jesus anzubeten
Les bergers viennent adorer Jésus
Los pastores van a adorar a Jesús

↑
Wise men from the East bring gifts for Jesus
Weise aus dem Morgenland bringen Jesus Geschenke
Des mages venus d'Orient apportent des présents à Jésus
Los Reyes Magos traen presentes a Jesús

↑↑

Jesus is circumcised
Jesus wird beschnitten
Circoncision de Jésus
Jesús es circuncidado

↑

Wise men from the East bring gifts for Jesus
Weise aus dem Morgenland bringen Jesus Geschenke
Des mages venus d'Orient apportent des présents à Jésus
Los Reyes Magos traen presentes a Jesús

↑

Simeon blesses Jesus in the temple
Simeon segnet Jesus im Tempel
Syméon bénit Jésus dans le temple
Simeón bendice a Jesús en el Templo

↑

Wise men from the East bring gifts for Jesus
Weise aus dem Morgenland bringen Jesus Geschenke
Des mages venus d'Orient apportent des présents à Jésus
Los Reyes Magos traen presentes a Jesús

↑ →

Wise men from the East bring gifts for Jesus
Weise aus dem Morgenland bringen Jesus Geschenke
Des mages venus d'Orient apportent des présents à Jésus
Los Reyes Magos traen presentes a Jesús

← ⇑

Joseph and his family escape to Egypt
Josef und seine Familie fliehen nach Ägypten
Joseph et sa famille s'enfuient en Egypte
José y su familia huyen a Egipto

↑

Herod kills all the baby boys in Bethlehem
Herodes lässt alle Knaben bis 2 Jahre in Bethlehem töten
Hérode fait tuer tous les bébés mâles de Bethléem
Herodes mata a todos los niños de Belén

↑
Joseph and his family escape to Egypt
Josef und seine Familie fliehen nach Ägypten
Joseph et sa famille s'enfuient en Egypte
José y su familia huyen a Egipto

→
Jesus in the temple, talking with the teachers
Jesus redet im Tempel mit Gesetzeslehrern
Jésus au temple, parlant avec les maîtres
Jesús habla en el Templo con los doctores de la Ley

↟ ↑

Jesus in the temple talking with the teachers
Jesus redet im Tempel mit Gesetzeslehrern
Jésus au temple, parlant avec les maîtres
Jesús habla en el Templo con los doctores de la Ley

↑ | ↑

John the Baptist preaching in the wilderness
Johannes der Täufer predigt in der Wildnis
Jean le Baptiste prêchant dans le désert
San Juan el Bautista predicando en el desierto

John the Baptist baptises Jesus
Johannes der Täufer tauft Jesus
Jean le Baptiste baptise Jésus
San Juan el Bautista bautiza a Jesús

61

↑

John the Baptist baptizes Jesus
Johannes der Täufer tauft Jesus
Jean le Baptiste baptise Jésus
San Juan el Bautista bautiza a Jesús

↑ →

The devil tempts Jesus in the wilderness
Der Teufel versucht Jesus in der Wildnis
Le diable tente Jésus dans le désert
El demonio tienta a Jesús en el desierto

 Jesus turns water into wine at a wedding at Cana in Galilee
Jesus verwandelt bei einer Hochzeit im galiläischen Kana Wasser in Wein
Jésus change l'eau en vin lors d'une noce à Cana de Galilée
Jesús convierte agua en vino en una boda en Caná de Galilea

 Nicodemus comes to Jesus at night
Nikodemus kommt nachts zu Jesus
Nicodème vient, de nuit, trouver Jésus
Nicodemo va a ver a Jesús de noche

↑

Jesus turns water into wine at a wedding at Cana in Galilee
Jesus verwandelt bei einer Hochzeit im galiläischen Kana Wasser in Wein
Jésus change l'eau en vin lors d'une noce à Cana de Galilée
Jesús convierte agua en vino en una boda en Caná de Galilea

↑

Nicodemus comes to Jesus at night
Nikodemus kommt nachts zu Jesus
Nicodème vient, de nuit, trouver Jésus
Nicodemo va a ver a Jesús de noche

↑ →
Jesus and a Samaritan woman at Jacob's well
Jesus und eine Samariterin am Jakobsbrunnen
Jésus et une Samaritaine au puits de Jacob
Jesús y una samaritana en el pozo de Jacob

 Jesus calls 4 fishermen to be disciples: Peter, Andrew, James and John
Jesus beruft 4 Fischer zu Jüngern: Petrus, Andreas, Jakobus und Johannes
Jésus appelle 4 pêcheurs à être ses disciples : Pierre, André, Jacques & Jean
Jesús nombra discípulos a 4 pescadores: Pedro, Andrés, Santiago y Juan

↑ Jesus heals Peter's mother-in-law and many other sick people
Jesus heilt Petrus' Schwiegermutter und viele andere Menschen
Jésus guérit la belle-mère de Simon et beaucoup d'autres
Jesús sana a la suegra de Pedro y a muchos otros

↑   ↑

Jesus calls 4 fishermen to be disciples: Peter, Andrew, James and John
Jesus beruft 4 Fischer zu Jüngern: Petrus, Andreas, Jakobus und Johannes
Jésus appelle 4 pêcheurs à être ses disciples : Pierre, André, Jacques & Jean
Jesús nombra discípulos a 4 pescadores: Pedro, Andrés, Santiago y Juan

Jesus performs many miracles, healing many sick people
Jesus bewirkt viele Wunder und Heilungen
Jésus accomplit des miracles en guérissant de nombreux malades
Jesús obra milagros y sana a muchas personas

↑
Jesus performs many miracles, healing many sick people
Jesus bewirkt viele Wunder und Heilungen
Jésus accomplit des miracles en guérissant de nombreux malades
Jesús obra milagros y sana a muchas personas

→
A miraculous catch of fish
Der wunderbare Fischzug
Une pêche miraculeuse
La pesca milagrosa

Jesus heals a leper near Capernaum
Jesus heilt einen Aussätzigen bei Kafarnaum
Jésus guérit un lépreux à Capharnaüm
Jesús sana a un leproso en Cafarnaúm

A paralysed man is lowered through the roof to Jesus
Ein Gelähmter wird durchs Dach zu Jesus herabgelassen
Un paralytique est descendu à travers le toit pour être présenté à Jésus
Bajan por el tejado a un paralítico hasta Jesús

The Rt. Worshipfull St.Tho: Mompesson of Bathampton in Wiltshire Knight For the Advancement of this Work Contributed this Plate, to whose Patronage it is humbly dedicated by Richard Blome

 A paralysed man is lowered through the roof to Jesus
Ein Gelähmter wird durchs Dach zu Jesus herabgelassen
Un paralytique est descendu à travers le toit pour être présenté à Jésus
Bajan por el tejado a un paralítico hasta Jesús

 Jesus calls Matthew, the tax collector, to be a disciple
Jesus beruft den Steuereintreiber Matthäus zum Jünger
Jésus appelle Matthieu, le collecteur d'impôts, à être un disciple
Jesús nombra discípulo a Mateo, el publicano

<table>
<tr><td align="center">↑</td><td align="center">↑</td></tr>
</table>

↑   ↑

Jesus calls Matthew, the tax collector, to be a disciple
Jesus beruft den Steuereintreiber Matthäus zum Jünger
Jésus appelle Matthieu, le collecteur d'impôts, à être un disciple
Jesús nombra discípulo a Mateo, el publicano

Jesus heals a man at the pool called Bethesda
Jesus heilt einen Mann am Teich Betesda
Jésus guérit un paralytique à la piscine appelée Bethesda
Jesús sana a un paralítico en la piscina de Betesda

Jesus heals a man at the pool called Bethesda
Jesus heilt einen Mann am Teich Betesda
Jésus guérit un paralytique à la piscine appelée Bethesda
Jesús sana a un paralítico en la piscina de Betesda

↑   ↑

The disciples are rebuked for picking grain on the Sabbath
Die Jünger werden kritisiert, weil sie am Sabbat Korn pflücken
Les disciples sont invectivés pour avoir arraché des épis le jour de Sabbat
Los discípulos son criticados por recoger espigas en sábado

So many gather that Jesus withdraws to a boat to preach
Es versammeln sich so viele, dass Jesus vom Boot aus predigt
Devant la foule nombreuse, Jésus se retire sur une barque pour prêcher
Se juntan tantos que Jesús se sube a una barca para predicar

 Jesus is criticised for healing a woman on the Sabbath
Jesus wird kritisiert, weil er am Sabbat eine Frau heilt
Jésus invectivé pour avoir guéri une femme le jour de Sabbat
Jesús es censurado por sanar a una mujer en sábado

 Jesus selects the 12 apostles
Jesus wählt die 12 Apostel aus
Jésus choisit les 12 apôtres
Jesús elige a los 12 apóstoles

↑

Jesus selects the 12 apostles
Jesus wählt die 12 Apostel aus
Jésus choisit les 12 apôtres
Jesús elige a los 12 apóstoles

↑

The Sermon on the Mount
Die Predigt am Berg
Prédication sur la montagne
El sermón de la montaña

The Sermon on the Mount
Die Predigt am Berg
Prédication sur la montagne
El sermón de la montaña

You see the speck in your brother's eye, but not the plank in your own
Den Splitter im Auge seines Bruders sehen, doch nicht den Balken im eigenen Auge
Tu vois la paille dans l'œil de ton frère mais pas la poutre dans ton œil à toi
Ves la paja en el ojo ajeno pero no la viga en el tuyo

The Rt. Worshipfull Sr. Thomas Fitch of
Eltham & Mount = Mascall in Kent Kt.
& Baronet, a descen= dant of ye antiant
Family of ye Fitches of Fitches Castle
in the North.

For ye advancment of this work, contributed
this Plate to Whose Patronage it is humbly
dedicated by Richard Blome.

Jesus heals a centurion's servant
Jesus heilt den Diener eines Hauptmanns
Jésus guérit l'esclave d'un centurion
Jesús sana al siervo de un centurión

Jesus brings a widow's son back to life
Jesus erweckt den Sohn einer Witwe wieder zum Leben
Jésus ramène le fils d'une veuve à la vie
Jesús resucita al hijo de una viuda

Mary Magdalene washes Jesus' feet
Maria aus Magdala wäscht Jesu Füße
Marie-Madeleine lave les pieds de Jésus
María Magdalena lava los pies a Jesús

Mary Magdalene washes Jesus' feet
Maria aus Magdala wäscht Jesu Füße
Marie-Madeleine lave les pieds de Jésus
María Magdalena lava los pies a Jesús

Jesus preaches the parable of the sower from a boat
Jesus predigt vom Boot aus - das Gleichnis von der Aussaat
Jésus prêche depuis un bateau & la parabole de la semence
Jesús predica la parábola del sembrador desde una barca

↑

Jesus calms the stormy sea
Jesus gebietet Sturm und Wellen Einhalt
Jésus apaise une tempête
Jesús calma la tempestad del lago

↑

Demons driven out of a man's body enter a herd of pigs
Böse Geister fahren aus dem Leib eines Mannes in eine Schweineherde
Démons sortant d'un homme et entrant dans un troupeau de porcs
Los demonios expulsados de un hombre entran en una piara

85

Jesus calms the stormy sea

Demons driven out of a man's body enter a herd of pigs

Jesus gebietet Sturm und Wellen Einhalt

Böse Geister fahren aus dem Leib eines Mannes in eine Schweineherde

Jésus apaise une tempête

Démons sortant du corps d'un homme et entrant dans un troupeau de porcs

Jesús calma la tempestad del lago

Los demonios expulsados de un hombre entran en una piara

Jesus brings Jairus' daughter back to life
Jesus erweckt Jaïrus' Tochter wieder zum Leben
Jésus ramène la fille de Jaïros à la vie
Jesús resucita a la hija de Jairo

A woman is healed when she touches Jesus' clothing
Eine Frau wird geheilt, als sie Jesu Kleidung berührt
Une femme est guérie en touchant le vêtement de Jésus
Una mujer se cura al tocar el manto de Jesús

⇑

↑

Jairus asks Jesus to heal his daughter
Jaïrus bittet Jesus, seine Tochter zu heilen
Jaïros supplie Jésus de guérir sa fille
Jairo pide a Jesús que sane a su hija

Jesus sends the 12 apostles to preach
Jesus schickt die 12 Apostel predigen
Jésus envoie les 12 apôtres prêcher
Jesús envía a predicar a los 12 apóstoles

Demons driven out of a man's body enter a herd of pigs
Böse Geister fahren aus dem Leib eines Mannes in eine Schweineherde
Démons sortant du corps d'un homme et entrant dans un troupeau de porcs
Los demonios expulsados de un hombre entran en una piara

John the Baptist is killed
Johannes der Täufer wird getötet
Jean le Baptiste est tué
Matan a san Juan el Bautista

↑

Herodias asks for John the Baptist's head on a platter
Herodias fordert den Kopf von Johannes dem Täufer
Hérode demande la tête de Jean le Baptiste sur un plateau
Herodes pide la cabeza de Juan el Bautista en una bandeja

Herodias asks for John the Baptist's head on a platter
Herodias fordert den Kopf von Johannes dem Täufer
Hérode demande la tête de Jean le Baptiste sur un plateau
Herodes pide la cabeza de Juan el Bautista en una bandeja

Jesus feeds 5000 people with 5 loaves and 2 fish
Jesus sättigt 5000 Menschen mit 5 Brotlaiben und 2 Fischen
Jésus nourrit 5000 personnes avec 5 pains et 2 poissons
Jesús alimenta a 5.000 hombres con 5 panes y 2 peces

Jesus walks on water and Peter tries to walk out to him
Jesus geht auf dem Wasser; Petrus versucht, zu ihm zu gehen
Jésus marche sur l'eau et Pierre essaie de le rejoindre
Jesús camina sobre las aguas y Pedro trata de unirse a él

The Right Hon.ble Charles Montague
Earle of Manchester. Vifcount Mandevill
Baron of Kimbolton etc.
For the Advancement of this Worke
Contributed this Plate to whofe
Patronage it is Humbly Dedicated
By Richard Blome

Jesus feeds 5000 people with 5 loaves and 2 fish
Jesus sättigt 5000 Menschen mit 5 Brotlaiben und 2 Fischen
Jésus nourrit 5000 personnes avec 5 pains et 2 poissons
Jesús alimenta a 5.000 hombres con 5 panes y 2 peces

Jesus walks on water and Peter tries to walk out to him
Jesus geht auf dem Wasser; Petrus versucht, zu ihm zu gehen
Jésus marche sur l'eau et Pierre essaie de le rejoindre
Jesús camina sobre las aguas y Pedro trata de unirse a él

96

← ↟ ↑ →

The transfiguration of Jesus, in the presence of Moses and Elijah
Die Verklärung Jesu in Gegenwart von Mose und Elija
La transfiguration de Jésus, en la présence de Moïse et Elie
La Transfiguración de Jesús, en presencia de Moisés y Elías

 →

The one who is least among you is the one who is great
Wer unter euch der Allergeringste ist, der ist groß
Celui qui est le plus petit d'entre vous tous, voilà le plus grand
El más pequeño de entre vosotros, ese es mayor

An adulterous woman is brought to Jesus
Eine Ehebrecherin wird vor Jesus gebracht
Une femme adultère est amenée à Jésus
Llevan a Jesús una mujer sorprendida en adulterio

 Jesus describes himself as the good shepherd
Jesus spricht von sich als einem guten Hirten
Jésus se décrit comme le bon berger
Jesús se autodenomina el buen Pastor

↑

Jesus describes himself as the good shepherd
Jesus spricht von sich als einem guten Hirten
Jésus se décrit comme le bon berger
Jesús se autodenomina el buen Pastor

↑

Parable of the good Samaritan
Gleichnis vom barmherzigen Samariter
Parabole du bon Samaritain
Parábola del buen samaritano

Parable of the good Samaritan: a priest and a Levite pass without helping
Gleichnis vom barmherzigen Samariter: Priester und Levit gehen weiter
Parabole du bon Samaritain : un prêtre et un lévite passent
Parábola del buen samaritano: un sacerdote y un levita pasan de largo

Parable of the good Samaritan: the Samaritan helps the injured man
Gleichnis vom barmherzigen Samariter: Der Samariter hilft dem Verletzten
Parabole du bon Samaritain : le Samaritain porte secours à l'homme blessé
Parábola del buen samaritano: el samaritano ayuda al herido

104

Parable of the good Samaritan
Gleichnis vom barmherzigen Samariter
Parabole du bon Samaritain
Parábola del buen samaritano

Martha prepares a meal while Mary listens to Jesus
Marta bereitet das Mahl, während Maria Jesus zuhört
Marthe prépare le repas tandis que Marie écoute Jésus
Marta hace la comida mientras María escucha a Jesús

Martha prepares a meal while Mary listens to Jesus
Marta bereitet das Mahl, während Maria Jesus zuhört
Marthe prépare le repas tandis que Marie écoute Jésus
Marta hace la comida mientras María escucha a Jesús

Parable of the prodigal son: a son wastes his inheritance
Gleichnis vom verlorenen Sohn: Der Sohn verjubelt sein Erbe
Parabole du fils prodigue : un fils dilapide son héritage
Parábola del hijo pródigo: un hijo despilfarra toda su herencia

↑

Parable of the prodigal son: the son has nothing
Gleichnis vom verlorenen Sohn: Der Sohn ist bettelarm
Parabole du fils prodigue : le fils est dans le dénuement
Parábola del hijo pródigo: el hijo se hunde en la miseria

↑

Parable of the prodigal son: his father welcomes him home
Gleichnis vom verlorenen Sohn: Der Vater heißt ihn zuhause willkommen
Parabole du fils prodigue : son père l'accueille dans sa maison
Parábola del hijo pródigo: el padre le acoge nuevamente

Parable of the prodigal son: the son has nothing
Gleichnis vom verlorenen Sohn: Der Sohn ist bettelarm
Parabole du fils prodigue : le fils est dans le dénuement
Parábola del hijo pródigo: el hijo se hunde en la miseria

Parable of the prodigal son: his father welcomes him home
Gleichnis vom verlorenen Sohn: Der Vater heißt ihn zuhause willkommen
Parabole du fils prodigue : son père l'accueille dans sa maison
Parábola del hijo pródigo: el padre le acoge nuevamente

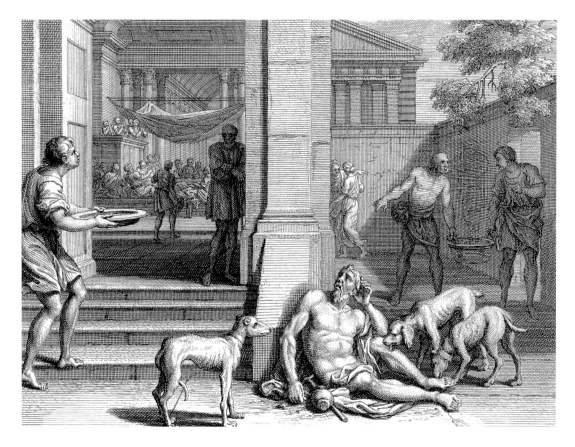

↑

↑

Parable of the rich man and Lazarus: Lazarus begs outside the temple
Gleichnis vom reichen Mann und Lazarus: Lazarus bettelt vor dem Tempel
Parabole du riche et de Lazare : Lazare mendiant devant le temple
Parábola del hombre rico y Lázaro: Lázaro mendiga fuera del Templo

Lazarus in heaven; the rich man is in hell
Lazarus sitzt im Himmel, der Reiche in der Hölle
Lazare au paradis ; le riche en enfer
Lázaro en el cielo y el rico en el infierno

111

Parable of the rich man and Lazarus
Gleichnis vom reichen Mann und armen Lazarus
Parabole du riche et de Lazare
Parábola del hombre rico y Lázaro

Better to be thrown into the sea than to cause a child to sin
Besser ins Meer geworfen werden, als auch nur einen Menschen irrezumachen
Mieux vaut être jeté à la mer que de faire tomber un seul des petits
Mejor ser arrojado al mar que hacer pecar a un niño

Jesus raises Lazarus from the dead
Jesus erweckt Lazarus von den Toten auf
Jésus ressuscite Lazare
Jesús resucita a Lázaro

Parable of the Pharisee and the tax collector
Gleichnis vom Pharisäer und vom Zöllner
Parabole du Pharisien et du collecteur d'impôts
Parábola del fariseo y el publicano

Jesus raises Lazarus from the dead
Jesus erweckt Lazarus von den Toten auf
Jésus ressuscite Lazare
Jesús resucita a Lázaro

Jesus says: Let the little children come unto me
Jesus sagt: Lasst die Kinder zu mir kommen
Jésus dit : Laissez les enfants venir à moi
Jesús dice: Dejad que los niños vengan a mí

Jesus says: Let the little children come unto me
Jesus sagt: Lasst die Kinder zu mir kommen
Jésus dit : Laissez les enfants venir à moi
Jesús dice: Dejad que los niños vengan a mí

A wealthy young ruler is saddened by Jesus' words
Ein junger Reicher geht betrübt über Jesu Worte davon
Un jeune notable riche part, attristé par les paroles de Jésus
Un joven dignatario rico se va muy triste por las palabras de Jesús

Parable of the workers in the vineyard
Gleichnis von den Arbeitern im Weinberg
Parabole des ouvriers dans la vigne
Parábola de los obreros de la viña

Jesus meets Zacchaeus in Jericho
Jesus begegnet Zachäus bei Jericho
Jésus rencontre Zachée à Jéricho
Jesús conoce a Zaqueo en Jericó

 Jesus heals a blind man near Jericho
Jesus heilt einen Blinden bei Jericho
Jésus guérit un aveugle près de Jéricho
Jesús sana a un ciego de Jericó

↑ Jesus meets Zacchaeus in Jericho
Jesus begegnet Zachäus bei Jericho
Jésus rencontre Zachée près de Jéricho
Jesús conoce a Zaqueo en Jericó

↑

Jesus enters Jerusalem on Palm Sunday
Jesus kommt am Palmsonntag nach Jerusalem
Jésus entre dans Jérusalem le dimanche des Rameaux
Jesús entra en Jerusalén el Domingo de Ramos

↑

Jesus drives the merchants out of the temple
Jesus treibt die Händler aus dem Tempel
Jésus chasse les marchands hors du temple
Jesús expulsa del Templo a los vendedores

121

 Jesus enters Jerusalem on Palm Sunday
Jesus kommt am Palmsonntag nach Jerusalem
Jésus entre dans Jérusalem le dimanche des Rameaux
Jesús entra en Jerusalén el Domingo de Ramos

↑ Jesus curses a fig tree for not bearing fruit
Jesus verflucht einen Feigenbaum ohne Früchte
Jésus maudit un figuier stérile
Jesús maldice la higuera estéril

↑↑   ↑

Parable of the tenants who kill the land-owner's son   Parable of the wedding banquet: the improperly dressed guest
Gleichnis von den bösen Weingärtnern   *Gleichnis vom schlecht gekleideten Hochzeitsgast*
Parabole des vignerons meurtriers du fils du maître de la vigne   Parabole du festin nuptial et de l'invité ne portant pas de vêtement de noce
Parábola de los viñadores homicidas   *Parábola del hombre mal vestido para una boda*

Pharisees question Jesus on paying taxes to Caesar
Die Pharisäer fragen Jesus nach der Steuer für den Kaiser
Les pharisiens interrogent Jésus à propos de l'impôt dû à César
Los fariseos preguntan a Jesús por el tributo debido al César

The widow's offering
Das Scherflein der Witwe
L'offrande de la veuve
El óbolo de la viuda

 ↑

Parable of the wise and foolish virgins at the wedding banquet
Gleichnis von den klugen und törichten Brautjungfern
Parabole des vierges insensées et des vierges avisées au banquet de noce
Parábola de las vírgenes prudentes y las necias en la boda

→

Parable of the talents
Gleichnis von den anvertrauten Talenten
Parabole des talents
Parábola de los talentos

The Honourable William Penn of
Worminghurst place in Sussex Esq.
Proprietor and Gouernour of the
Province of Pennsilvania in America

For ẏ Advancement of this ẏ worke Contributed this Plate &c
whose Patronage it is humbly Dedicated by
Richard Blome.

127

↑
Parable of the talents: Well done, my good and faithful servant
Gleichnis von den anvertrauten Talenten: Sehr gut, du bist ein tüchtiger und treuer Diener
Parabole des talents : C'est bien, bon et fidèle serviteur
Parábola de los talentos: bien hecho, siervo bueno y fiel

↑

Jesus said: I was hungry and you gave me food
Jesus sagt: Ich war hungrig und ihr habt mir zu essen gegeben
Jésus dit : j'ai eu faim et vous m'avez donné à manger
Jesús dijo: tuve hambre y me disteis de comer

↑

Jesus said: I was thirsty and you gave me something to drink
Jesus sagt: Ich war durstig und ihr habt mir zu trinken gegeben
Jésus dit : j'ai eu soif et vous m'avez donné à boire
Jesús dijo: tuve sed y me disteis de beber

Jesus said: I was a stranger and you invited me in
Jesus sagt: Ich war fremd und ihr habt mich bei euch aufgenommen
Jésus dit : j'étais un étranger et vous m'avez accueilli
Jesús dijo: era forastero y me acogisteis

Jesus said: I was naked and you gave me clothing
Jesus sagt: Ich war nackt und ihr habt mir etwas anzuziehen gegeben
Jésus dit : j'étais nu et vous m'avez vêtu
Jesús dijo: estaba desnudo y me vestisteis

↑

Jesus said: I was sick and you took care of me
Jesus sagt: Ich war krank und ihr habt mich versorgt
Jésus dit : j'étais malade et vous m'avez visité
Jesús dijo: estaba enfermo y me visitasteis

↑

Jesus said: I was in prison and you visited me
Jesus sagt: Ich war im Gefängnis und ihr habt mich besucht
Jésus dit : j'étais en prison et vous êtes venu à moi
Jesús dijo: estaba en la cárcel y vinisteis a verme

↟
A woman anoints Jesus with expensive oil from an alabaster jar
Eine Frau salbt Jesus mit sehr wertvollem Öl
Une femme oint Jésus d'un parfum cher contenu dans un flacon en albâtre
Una mujer unge a Jesús con perfume de un frasco de alabastro

↑
Judas agrees to betray Jesus for 30 silver coins
Judas verrät Jesus für 30 Silberstücke
Judas trahit Jésus pour 30 pièces d'argent
Judas traiciona a Jesús por 30 monedas de plata

Judas betrays Jesus for 30 silver coins
Judas verrät Jesus für 30 Silberstücke
Judas trahit Jésus pour 30 pièces d'argent
Judas traiciona a Jesús por 30 monedas de plata

Jesus washes the feet of the disciples
Jesus wäscht seinen Jüngern die Füße
Jésus lave les pieds des disciples
Jesús lava los pies de sus discípulos

↑

Jesus washes the feet of the disciples
Jesus wäscht seinen Jüngern die Füße
Jésus lave les pieds des disciples
Jesús lava los pies de sus discípulos

↑ →

The last supper
Das Abendmahl
La Cène
La última cena

↑

The last supper
Das Abendmahl
La Cène
La última cena

↑ →

Jesus in the garden of Gethsemanev
Jesus im Garten Getsemani
Jésus dans le jardin de Gethsémani
Jesús en el jardín de Getsemaní

↑

Jesus prays in the garden of Gethsemane
Jesus betet im Garten im Garten Getsemani
Jésus prie dans le jardin de Gethsémani
Jesús reza en Getsemaní

↑

A crowd appears to arrest Jesus
Eine Schar kommt Jesus festzunehmen
Une troupe apparaît pour arrêter Jésus
Un grupo llega para arrestar a Jesús

↟

↑

Judas betrays Jesus with a kiss: Peter cuts off Malchus' ear
Judas verrät Jesus mit einem Kuss: Petrus schlägt Malchus' Ohr ab
Judas trahit Jésus en lui donnant un baiser : Pierre coupe l'oreille de Malchus
Judas besa a Jesús y le entrega; Pedro corta la oreja a Malco

Jesus heals Malchus' ear
Jesus heilt Malchus' Ohr
Jésus guérit l'oreille de Malchus
Jesús sana la oreja de Malco

Jesus prays in the garden of Gethsemane: Father, take this cup from me
Jesus betet im Garten Getsemani: Vater, lass diesen Kelch an mir vorübergehen
Jésus priant dans le jardin de Gethsémani : Père, écarte de moi cette coupe
Jesús ora en Getsemaní: Padre, si quieres, aparta de mí esta copa

Jesus speaks to the crowd and they fall to the ground
Jesus spricht zu den Häschern und sie fallen zu Boden
Jésus parle à la foule et celle-ci tombe à terre
Jesús habla a los miembros del grupo y ellos caen al suelo

Peter disowns Jesus three times, just as Jesus predicted
Wie von Jesus prophezeit, verleugnet Petrus ihn drei Mal
Pierre renie trois fois Jésus, comme Jésus l'avait prédit
Pedro niega a Jesús tres veces, como este había predicho

↑
Judas tries to return the money he received for betraying Jesus
Judas will sein an Jesu Verrat verdientes Geld zurückgeben
Judas essaie de rendre l'argent qu'il a reçu pour trahir Jésus
Judas intenta devolver el dinero que cobró por vender a Jesús

↑
Jesus is brought before Pilate
Jesus wird vor Pilatus gebracht
Jésus traduit devant Pilate
Jesús es llevado ante Pilato

↑

Jesus is beaten

Jesus wird geschlagen

Jésus est battu

Jesús es golpeado

↑

Soldiers crown Jesus with thorns and mock him

Soldaten setzen Jesus eine Dornenkrone auf und verspotten ihn

Des soldats coiffent Jésus d'une couronne d'épines et se moquent de lui

Los soldados coronan a Jesús con espinas y se mofan de él

143

Judas kills himself after trying to return the 30 silver coins
Judas will die 30 Silberstücke zurückgeben und erhängt sich dann
Judas se tue après avoir tenté de rendre les 30 pièces d'argent
Judas se ahorca tras intentar devolver las 30 monedas de plata

Pilate tries to free Jesus; Jesus is beaten
Pilatus will Jesus freilassen; Jesus wird ausgepeitscht
Pilate essaie de libérer Jésus ; Jésus est flagellé
Pilato intenta liberar a Jesús; este es azotado

↑
Jesus is brought before Pilate
Jesus wird vor Pilatus gebracht
Jésus traduit devant Pilate
Jesús es llevado ante Pilato

Jesus is brought before Herod
Jesus wird vor Herodes gebracht
Jésus est conduit devant Hérode
Jesús es llevado ante Herodes

Pilate washes his hands before the crowd
Pilatus wäscht sich vor dem Volk die Hände
Pilate se lave les mains devant la foule
Pilato se lava las manos ante la multitud

↑   ↑

Soldiers crown Jesus with thorns and mock him

Soldaten setzen Jesus eine Dornenkrone auf und verspotten ihn

Des soldats coiffent Jésus d'une couronne d'épines et se moquent de lui

Los soldados coronan a Jesús con espinas y se mofan de él

Pilate has Jesus flogged and delivers him to be crucified

Pilatus lässt Jesus auspeitschen und gibt ihn zur Kreuzigung frei

Pilate fait flageller Jésus et le livre pour être crucifié

Pilato hace azotar a Jesús y le entrega para que sea crucificado

Pilate washes his hands before the crowd
Pilatus wäscht sich vor dem Volk die Hände
Pilate se lave les mains devant la foule
Pilato se lava las manos ante la multitud

Jesus, wearing a crown of thorns, is mocked by the crowd
Jesus mit Dornenkrone wird von der Menge verspottet
Jésus, portant une couronne d'épines, tourné en ridicule par la foule
La multitud se burla de Jesús, coronado con espinas

↑
Jesus carries the cross to Golgotha helped by Simon of Cyrene: the picture alludes to the Turin Shroud
Jesus trägt das Kreuz nach Golgota; Simon von Zyrene will ihm helfen; mit Anspielung auf das Turiner Grabtuch
Jésus porte la croix à Golgotha ; Simon de Cyrène vient à son aide ; et allusion au suaire de Turin
Jesús carga con su cruz hasta el Gólgota; Simón de Cirene le ayuda y una alusión al Santo Sudario de Turín

↑

Jesus carries the cross to Golgotha
Jesus trägt das Kreuz nach Golgota
Jésus porte la croix à Golgotha
Jesús carga con su cruz hasta el Gólgota

↑

Jesus is crucified
Jesus wird ans Kreuz geschlagen
Jésus est crucifié
Jesús es crucificado

Simon of Cyrene carries the cross; Jesus speaks to a weeping woman
Simon von Zyrene trägt das Kreuz; Jesus spricht zu einer weinenden Frau
Simon de Cyrène porte la croix ; Jésus parle à une femme en pleurs
Simón de Cirene carga la cruz; Jesús se dirige a una mujer que llora

Jesus is crucified
Jesus wird ans Kreuz geschlagen
Jésus est crucifié
Jesús es crucificado

↑

Two criminals are crucified alongside Jesus
Kreuzigung von zwei Verbrechern neben Jesus
Deux malfaiteurs sont crucifiés à côté de Jésus
Dos malhechores son crucificados con Jesús

↑

Jesus' body is lowered from the cross
Jesu Leichnam wird vom Kreuz genommen
Le corps de Jésus est descendu de la croix
Bajan el cuerpo de Jesús de la cruz

↑ →
The crucifixion of Jesus
Jesu Kreuzigung
Jésus crucifié
La crucifixión de Jesús

154

↑

Jesus is thirsty and is given vinegar
Jesus ist durstig und bekommt Essig
Jésus a soif, on lui donne du vinaigre
Jesús tiene sed y le dan vinagre

The crucifixion of Jesus
Jesu Kreuzigung
Jésus crucifié
La crucifixión de Jesús

Jesus' body is lowered from the cross
Jesu Leichnam wird vom Kreuz genommen
Le corps de Jésus est descendu de la croix
Bajan el cuerpo de Jesús de la cruz

↑

The temple veil tears from top to bottom when Jesus dies
Der Vorhang im Tempel zerreißt in der Mitte, als Jesus stirbt
Le voile du sanctuaire se déchire par le milieu à la mort de Jésus
El velo del Santuario se rasga por el medio cuando Jesús muere

↑

The crucifixion of Jesus
Jesu Kreuzigung
Jésus crucifié
La crucifixión de Jesús

 ↑

Jesus' body is lowered from the cross
Jesu Leichnam wird vom Kreuz genommen
Le corps de Jésus est descendu de la croix
Bajan el cuerpo de Jesús de la cruz

↑

Jesus' body is placed in an empty tomb
Jesu Leichnam wird in ein neues Grab gelegt
Le corps de Jésus est déposé dans une tombe vide
Jesús es puesto en un sepulcro vacío

160

↑↑   ↑

Joseph of Arimathea takes charge of Jesus' body
Josef von Arimathäa kümmert sich um den Leichnam von Jesus
Joseph d'Arimathée se charge du corps de Jésus
José de Arimatea se hace cargo del cuerpo de Jesús

Angels appear to the 3 women who come to the tomb
Engel erscheinen den 3 Frauen am Grab
Des anges apparaissent aux 3 femmes venues au tombeau
Unos ángeles se aparecen a 3 mujeres que van al sepulcro

161

↑
Mary and the angels mourn Jesus' death
Maria und die Engel betrauern Jesu Tod
Marie et les anges pleurent la mort de Jésus
María y los ángeles lloran la muerte de Jesús

↑

Jesus' body is placed in an empty tomb
Jesu Leichnam wird ins Grab gelegt
Le corps de Jésus est déposé dans une nouvelle tombe
El cuerpo de Jesús es puesto en el sepulcro

↑

Jesus rises from his grave
Jesus erhebt sich aus seinem Grab
Résurrection de Jésus
Resurrección de Jesús

163

↑
Jesus rises from his grave
Jesus erhebt sich aus seinem Grab
Résurrection de Jésus
Resurrección de Jesús

→
An angel appears to the women who come to the tomb
Ein Engel erscheint den Frauen am Grab
Un ange apparaît aux femmes venues au tombeau
Un ángel se aparece a las mujeres que van al sepulcro

 ↑

An angel appears to the women who come to the tomb
Ein Engel erscheint den Frauen am Grab
Un ange apparaît aux femmes venues au tombeau
Un ángel se aparece a las mujeres que van al sepulcro

Peter and John inspect Jesus' empty tomb
Petrus und Johannes sehen das leere Grab Jesu
Pierre et Jean inspectent le tombeau vide de Jésus
Pedro y Juan revisan el sepulcro vacío

↑   ↑ ⇥

Jesus appears to Mary Magdalene
Jesus erscheint Maria aus Magdala
Jésus apparaît à Marie-Madeleine
Jesús se aparece a María Magdalena

Jesus appears to 2 disciples on the road to Emmaus
Jesus erscheint 2 Jüngern auf dem Weg nach Emmaus
Jésus révèle son identité aux 2 disciples à Emmaüs
Jesús se aparece a 2 discípulos en el camino a Emaús

↟   ↑

Jesus appears to Mary Magdalene   Jesus reveals His identity to the 2 disciples in Emmaus
Jesus erscheint Maria aus Magdala   *Jesus gibt sich den 2 Jüngern in Emmaus zu erkennen*
Jésus apparaît à Marie-Madeleine   Jésus révèle son identité aux 2 disciples à Emmaüs
Jesús se aparece a María Magdalena   *Jesús revela su identidad a los 2 discípulos en Emaús*

169

↑

Jesus appears to the disciples in Jerusalem
Jesus erscheint den Jüngern in Jerusalem
Jésus apparaît aux disciples à Jérusalem
Jesús se aparece a los discípulos en Jerusalén

↑

Thomas doubts and touches Jesus' wounds
Der zweifelnde Thomas berührt Jesu Wunden
Thomas doute et touche les plaies de Jésus
Tomás duda y toca las heridas de Jesús

Thomas doubts and touches Jesus' wounds
Der zweifelnde Thomas berührt Jesu Wunden
Thomas doute et touche les plaies de Jésus
Tomás duda y toca las heridas de Jesús

Jesus appears to 7 disciples by the Sea of Tiberias
Jesus erscheint 7 Jüngern am See von Tiberias
Jésus apparaît aux 7 disciples sur les bords de la mer Tibériade
Jesús se aparece a 7 discípulos junto al lago de Tiberíades

↑ →
Jesus is taken up into heaven
Jesus wird zum Himmel emporgehoben
Jésus est emporté au ciel
Jesús es llevado al cielo

172

 ↑ →

Jesus is taken up into heaven
Jesus wird zum Himmel emporgehoben
Jésus est emporté au ciel
Jesús es llevado al cielo

The Holy Spirit comes at Pentecost
Der Heilige Geist erscheint an Pfingsten
Venue du Saint Esprit à la Pentecôte
El Espíritu Santo viene en Pentecostés

← The Holy Spirit comes at Pentecost
Der Heilige Geist erscheint an Pfingsten
Venue du Saint Esprit à la Pentecôte
El Espíritu Santo viene en Pentecostés

↑
Mary Magdalene, the penitent
Maria aus Magdala als Büßerin
Marie-Madeleine, repentante
María Magdalena, la penitente

↑ Map: the travels of the apostles and in particular of Paul
Karte: Die Reisen der Apostel, speziell von Paulus
Carte : les voyages des apôtres, en particulier ceux de Paul
Mapa: los viajes de los apóstoles y, en concreto, de Pablo

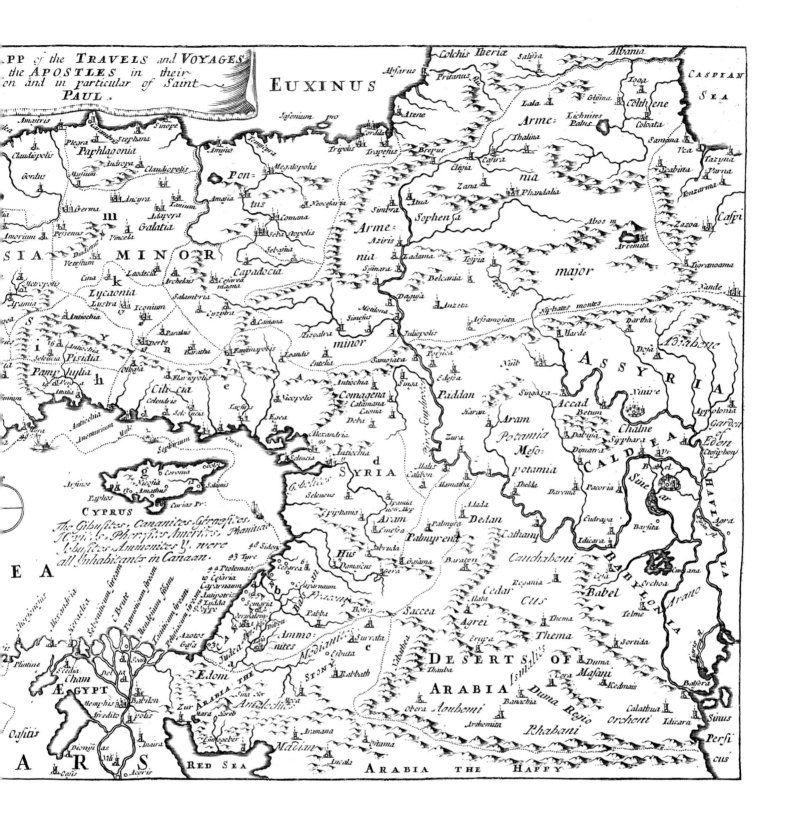

MAPP of the TRAVELS and VOYAGES of the APOSTLES in their Dispersion and in particular of Saint PAUL.

EUXINUS

CYPRUS

The Gibusites, Cananites, Gergesites, Hevites, Pherisites, Amorites, Jebusites, Ammonites &c. were all Inhabitants in Canaan.

179

 Ananias and Sapphira are struck dead for lying
Hananias und Saphira müssen für ihre Lüge sterben
Ananias et Saphira meurent pour avoir menti
Ananías y Safira mueren por mentir

↑ The sick believe that being touched by Peter's shadow will heal them
Die Kranken glauben, geheilt zu werden, wenn Petrus' Schatten auf sie fällt
Les malades croient que l'ombre de Pierre va les guérir
Los enfermos creen que se curarán si les toca la sombra de Pedro

↑

The Holy Spirit comes at Pentecost
Der Heilige Geist erscheint an Pfingsten
Venue du Saint Esprit à la Pentecôte
El Espíritu Santo viene en Pentecostés

↑

Peter and John heal a crippled man
Petrus und Johannes heilen einen Gelähmten
Pierre et Jean guérissent un infirme
Pedro y Juan curan a un tullido

The Honourable Hender Molesworth
Sqr Governour of his Majestys
Irland of Jamaica
Anno Domini 1687
For ye Advancement of
to Whose Patronage it is humbly this Worke contributed this Plate,
Dedicated by Richard Blome

↑
Peter and John heal a crippled man
Petrus und Johannes heilen einen Gelähmten
Pierre et Jean guérissent un infirme
Pedro y Juan curan a un tullido

↑
Ananias and Sapphira are struck dead for lying
Hananias und Saphira müssen für ihre Lüge sterben
Ananias et Saphira meurent pour avoir menti
Ananías y Safira mueren por mentir

↑
The apostles perform many miracles
Die Apostel bewirken viele Wunder
Les apôtres accomplissent des miracles
Los apóstoles obran muchos milagros

183

↑ →
Stephen is stoned
Stephanus wird gesteinigt
Etienne est lapidé
Esteban es lapidado

The Worshipfull Richard Cheyney of the parish of the County of For this Advancement this Plate to whose Dedicated by ... full Richard Hamerton in Hackney in Middlesex Esqß of this work Contributor Patronage it is humly Richard Blome

 Philip baptises an Ethiopian eunuch
Philippus tauft einen äthiopischen Eunuchen
Philippe baptise un eunuque éthiopien
Felipe bautiza a un eunuco etíope

→ Saul is struck down and blinded on the road to Damascus
Saulus wird auf der Straße nach Damaskus geblendet und stürzt
Saul tombe à terre et devient aveugle sur la route de Damas
Saulo cae a tierra y es cegado en el camino de Damasco

The R.t Hon.ble John
Gowran. Colonell
Streame Rigem.t
Cap.t Generall &
Wight Contable
Major Generall
Horse and

L.t Gutts, Baron of
of his Ma.ties Cold.
of English foot Guards
Governour of the Isle of
of Carsbrook Castle
of his Ma.ties Armies both
Foot &c.

SUDORE   ET   SANGUINE

For y.e Aduancement of this
Patronage it is most

Worke, Contributed this Plate to whose
Humbly dedicated by Richard Blome

Philip baptises an Ethiopian eunuch
Philippus tauft einen äthiopischen Eunuchen
Philippe baptise un eunuque éthiopien
Felipe bautiza a un eunuco etíope

Saul is struck down and blinded on the road to Damascus
Saulus wird auf der Straße nach Damaskus geblendet und stürzt
Saul tombe à terre et devient aveugle sur la route de Damas
Saulo cae a tierra y es cegado en el camino de Damasco

Ananias restores Saul's sight: Saul is converted and beomes Paul
Hananias stellt Saulus' Sehkraft wieder her; Saulus wird zu Paulus
Ananias rend la vue à Saul et Saul se convertit et devient Paul
Ananías devuelve la vista a Saulo, que se convierte y pasa a ser Pablo

Peter's vision of the unclean meat
Petrus' Vision vom unreinen Fleisch
Vision de Pierre de la viande impure
Visión de Pedro de la carne impura

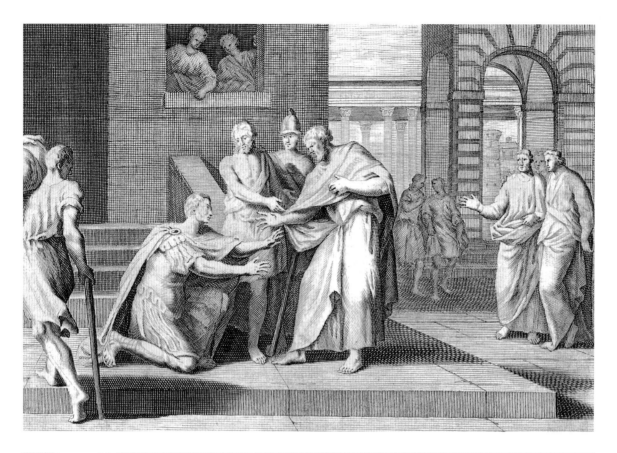

Peter baptises Cornelius, a centurion and gentile
Petrus tauft den nichtjüdischen Hauptmann Kornelius
Pierre baptise Corneille, un centurion et gentil
Pedro bautiza a Cornelio, un centurión gentil

An angel delivers Peter from prison
Ein Engel befreit Petrus aus dem Kerker
Un ange délivre Pierre de prison
Un ángel libra a Pedro de la cárcel

190

Paul blinds the magician Elymas
Paulus blendet den Magier Elymas
Paul rend aveugle le magicien Elymas
Pablo deja ciego al mago Elimas

Paul heals a lame man in Lystra
Paulus heilt einen Gelähmten in Lystra
Paul guérit un infirme à Lystre
Pablo cura a un tullido en Listra

The Right Honourable William Pierrepont, Earl of
Kingston upon Hull, Viscount
Newarke upon Trent and Baron of Holme
Pierrepont, Manvers, Norris &c.
For y. Advancement of this Worke, Contributed
this Plate, to whose Patronage it is humbly dedicated by
Richard Blome.

↑
An angel delivers Peter from prison
Ein Engel befreit Petrus aus dem Kerker
Un ange délivre Pierre de prison
Un ángel libra a Pedro de la cárcel

↑

Paul heals a lame man in Lystra
Paulus heilt einen Gelähmten in Lystra
Paul guérit un infirme à Lystre
Pablo cura a un tullido en Listra

↑ →
Books of magic are burned in Ephesus
In Ephesus werden Zauberbücher verbrannt
Des livres de magie sont brûlés à Ephèse
Queman libros de magia en Éfeso

↑
Eutychus falls to his death and Paul brings him back to life
Paulus erweckt den tödlich gestürzten Eutychus wieder zum Leben
Eutyque fait une chute mortelle et Paul le ramène à la vie
Eutico se mata al caer por la ventana y Pablo le resucita

 Paul speaks to the church elders of Ephesus
Paulus spricht zu den Gemeindeältesten von Ephesus
Paul parle aux anciens de l'Eglise d'Ephèse
Pablo habla a los ancianos de la iglesia de Éfeso

↑ Paul is interrogated in Jerusalem
Paulus wird in Jerusalem verhört
Paul est interrogé à Jérusalem
Pablo es interrogado en Jerusalén

↑↑

Paul is shipwrecked on Malta on his way to Rome
Paulus erleidet auf dem Weg nach Rom vor Malta Schiffbruch
En route vers Rome, Paul échoue à Malte
Pablo naufraga en Malta de camino a Roma

↑

Paul is bitten by a viper but is unharmed
Eine Viper beißt Paulus, dem aber nichts geschieht
Paul est mordu par une vipère mais est indemne
Una víbora muerde a Pablo pero no sufre daño alguno

197

↑   →

Paul, shipwrecked on Malta, is bitten by a viper but is not harmed

John of Patmos, the author of the *Book of Revelations*

Eine Viper beißt den auf Malta gestrandeten Paulus, doch geschieht ihm nichts

Johannes von Patmos, der das »Buch der Offenbarung« verfasste

Echoué à Malte, Paul est mordu par une vipère mais est indemne

Jean de Patmos, auteur du « Livre des Révélations »

Pablo, náufrago en Malta, es mordido por una víbora, pero no sufre daño alguno

Juan de Patmos, el autor del «Apocalipsis»

198

↑

A vision of hell
Eine Vision der Hölle
Une vision d'enfer
Visión del infierno

→

Judgement day
Der Tag des Jüngsten Gerichts
Jour du jugement
El día del Juicio Final

↑

An angel appears to John
Ein Engel erscheint Johannes
Un ange apparaît à Jean
Un ángel se aparece a Juan

→

A man with a sword coming out of his mouth and 7 golden lamps
Die Gestalt, aus deren Mund ein Schwert ragt, und 7 goldene Leuchter
Un homme avec un glaive dans la bouche & 7 chandeliers d'or
Un hombre de cuya boca sale una espada y 7 candeleros de oro

The Right Reverend Father in God Thomas Lord Bishop of
Rochester, Deane of Westminster & Clerke of the
Closet to his Ma.ty king James the 2d & ct
For the advancement of this Worke, Contributed this
Plate, to Whose Patronag it is Humbly dedicated, by
Richard Blome

203

 ↑

A man with a sword coming out of his mouth and 7 golden lamps
Die Gestalt, aus deren Mund ein Schwert ragt, und 7 goldene Leuchter
Un homme avec un glaive dans la bouche & 7 chandeliers d'or
Un hombre de cuya boca sale una espada y 7 candeleros de oro

The 24 thrones of the elders and 4 creatures giving eternal thanks
Die 24 Throne der Ältesten und 4 Wesen, die beständig Dank sagen
Les 24 trônes des anciens & 4 créatures rendant des actions de grâce
Los 24 tronos de los ancianos y los 4 seres alabando a Dios sin cesar

↑   ↑

A man with a sword coming out of his mouth and 7 golden lampstands   Heaven opens up and the throne of God appears
Die Gestalt, aus deren Mund ein Schwert ragt, und 7 goldene Leuchter   *Der Himmel öffnet sich und Gottes Thron erscheint*
Un homme avec un glaive dans la bouche & 7 chandeliers d'or   Le ciel s'ouvre et le trône de Dieu apparaît
Un hombre de cuya boca sale una espada y 7 candeleros de oro   *El cielo se abre y se muestra el trono de Dios*

 →

The lamb and the scroll with 7 seals
Das Lamm und die Rolle mit den 7 Siegeln
L'agneau et le livre et ses 7 sceaux
El Cordero y el libro con los 7 sellos

↑

The first 4 seals are opened: the 4 horsemen of the Apocalypse
Öffnung der ersten 4 Siegel: die 4 apokalyptischen Reiter
Les 4 premiers sceaux sont ouverts : les 4 chevaliers de l'Apocalypse
Los 4 primeros sellos se abren: los 4 jinetes del Apocalipsis

← ↑   ↑

The first 4 seals are opened: the 4 horsemen of the Apocalypse   The 5th seal opened: the souls of the martyrs cry out
Öffnung der ersten 4 Siegel: die 4 apokalyptischen Reiter   *Das 5. Siegel: Die Seelen der Märtyrer rufen*
Les 4 premiers sceaux sont ouverts : les 4 chevaliers de l'Apocalypse   5ème sceau : cris des âmes des martyres
Los 4 primeros sellos se abren: los 4 jinetes del Apocalipsis   *El 5.º sello: las almas de los mártires claman*

209

The 5th seal opened: the souls of the martyrs cry out
Das 5. Siegel: Die Seelen der Märtyrer rufen
5ème sceau : cris des âmes des martyres
El 5.º sello: las almas de los mártires claman

The 6th seal: the Sun turns black, the Moon red and the stars fall
Das 6. Siegel: Die Sonne wird schwarz, der Mond rot und die Sterne fallen herab
6ème sceau : le soleil devient noir, la lune rouge et les étoiles tombent
El 6.º sello: el sol ennegrece, la luna enrojece y las estrellas caen

↑   ↑

The 6th seal: the Sun turns black, the Moon red and the stars fall   The 7th seal: 7 angels with trumpets and another with a golden censer

Das 6. Siegel: Die Sonne wird schwarz, der Mond rot und die Sterne fallen herab   *Das 7. Siegel: 7 Engel mit Trompeten und einer mit goldenem Räuchergefäß*

6ème sceau : le soleil devient noir, la lune rouge et les étoiles tombent   7ème sceau : 7 anges avec des trompettes et 1 encensoir d'or

El 6.º sello: el sol ennegrece, la luna enrojece y las estrellas caen   *El 7.º sello: 7 ángeles con trompetas y uno con un incensario de oro*

↑

The 7th seal opened: 7 angels with trumpets and another with a golden incense burner who pours out fire on the Earth
Öffnung des 7. Siegels: 7 Engel trompeten; ein Engel mit goldenem Räuchergefäß gießt Feuer auf die Erde
7ème sceau ouvert : 7 anges avec des trompettes et un ange avec un encensoir d'or qui répand du feu sur la terre
El 7.º sello abierto: 7 ángeles con trompetas y otro con un incensario de oro que derrama fuego sobre la tierra

The Right Worshipfull
Sr. Robert Dashwood of
Norbrook in ye County of oxford Knight
for ye Advancement of this worke, Contributed this Plate, to whose
Patronage it is Humbly Dedicated by Richard Blome.

↑
The angel gives the little scroll (or book) to John to eat
Der Engel gibt Johannes eine kleine Handschrift zu essen
L'ange et le petit livre qui est donné à manger à Jean
El ángel le da el librito a Juan para que se lo coma

↑   →

The fate of the two witnesses who prophesy   Michael and his angels fight the dragon
Das Los der zwei prophetisch redenden Zeugen   *Michael mit seinen Engeln bekämpft den Drachen*
Le destin des deux témoins qui prophétisent   Michaël et ses anges combattent contre le dragon
Sino de los dos testigos que profetizan   *Miguel y sus ángeles combaten al dragón*

The woman of the Apocalypse, the child and the dragon
Die Frau aus der Apokalypse, das Kind und der Drache
La femme de l'Apocalypse, l'enfant et le dragon
La mujer del Apocalipsis, el hijo y el dragón

The whore Babylon riding the 7-headed beast
Die Hure Babylon reitet das 7-köpfige Tier
La prostituée Babylone chevauchant la bête aux 7 têtes
La Ramera de Babilonia sobre la bestia de 7 cabezas

The beast rising from the sea
Das Tier steigt aus dem Meer herauf
La bête surgissant de la mer
La Bestia surgiendo del mar

217

↑
Seven angels pour out God's wrath on the Earth
Sieben Engel gießen Gottes Zorn über die Erde aus
Sept anges répandent la colère de Dieu sur la terre
Siete ángeles derraman el furor de Dios sobre la tierra

↑

The beast rising from the sea
Das Tier steigt aus dem Meer herauf
La bête surgissant de la mer
La Bestia surgiendo del mar

↑

The lamb of God and the song of the 144,000
Das Lamm Gottes und das Lied der 144 000
L'agneau de Dieu et le cantique des 144000 rachetés
El Cordero de Dios y el cántico de los 144.000

↑

Seven angels pour out God's wrath on the earth
Sieben Engel gießen Gottes Zorn über die Erde aus
Sept anges répandent la colère de Dieu sur la terre
Siete ángeles derraman el furor de Dios sobre la tierra

↑ →

The fall of Babylon
Der Fall Babylons
Destruction de Babylone
La destrucción de Babilonia

Anne Lady Mason relict of Sr Richard
Mason of Worcester Park in Surrey, Knt
...of ye Clarks of ye Board of Gree...
...n cloth to his Maty King Charles ye 2. and
...dest daughter of Sr Iames Long
of Draycot:cerne in Wiltshire Baronet
For ye Advancement of this
...worke, Contributed this Plate...
to whose Patronage it is
...humbly Dedicated by
Richard Blome.

221

↑

The dragon is chained for 1000 years
Der Drache wird für 1000 Jahre angekettet
Le dragon est enchaîné pour mille ans
El Dragón es atado por 1.000 años

↑ →   ↑

The new Jerusalem descends from heaven   On either side of the river, the tree of life gives fruit all year
Das neue Jerusalem kommt vom Himmel herab   *Die Bäume des Lebens beiderseits des Flusses tragen das ganze Jahr Frucht*
La Jérusalem nouvelle descend du ciel   Au milieu des bras du fleuve, l'arbre de vie produisant 12 récoltes de fruits
La nueva Jerusalén desciende del cielo   *A una y otra margen del río, el árbol de la Vida da fruto 12 veces*